Do Not Read!

SPREAD GOOD VIBES JOURNAL

DAY-TO-DAY LIFE, THOUGHTS, AND FEELINGS

SHEBA BLAKE PUBLISHING CORP.
BROOKLYN NEW YORK

♥

CPSIA information can be obtained
at www.ICGtesting.com
Printed in the USA
LVHW080856210122
708837LV00020B/899